Using Media in the Classroom

Grades 4–5

by

Cathy Collison and Janis Campbell

Published by Instructional Fair
an imprint of
Frank Schaffer Publications®

About the Authors

Janis Campbell and Cathy Collison have been writing partners and friends for years. Between them, the two journalists have nearly forty years of experience. With the wide choice today of media—newspapers, magazines, television, radio, and the Internet—the authors think students need guidance more than ever on how to become smart media users.

Janis and Cathy write and edit together at the *Detroit Free Press*, where they produce a weekly newspaper magazine for young readers, *Yak's Corner*, which is delivered to families and classrooms throughout Michigan as part of the Newspaper in Education program. Yak's Corner is also a nationally syndicated feature running in nearly forty newspapers across the country. If Yak's Corner doesn't run in your paper, visit *www.yakscorner.com*.

Campbell and Collison have produced many teacher resources, including weekly lesson plans for Detroit teachers using *Yak's Corner* in the classroom. They have also been active volunteers in their children's school districts, keeping up to date with what students are doing in the classroom.

When they're not busy writing, they often are reading—newspapers, magazines, and media on the Web. They use the news to keep current and to stay informed. They hope you will teach your students to do so, too, with the help of this guide.

Instructional Fair

Authors: Cathy Collison and Janis Campbell
Editor: Diana Wallis
Cover Artist: Teather Uhrik
Interior Designer: Teather Uhrik

Frank Schaffer Publications®

Instructional Fair is an imprint of Frank Schaffer Publications.

Send all inquiries to:
Frank Schaffer Publications
3195 Wilson Drive NW
Grand Rapids, Michigan 49544

Using Media in the Classroom—grades 4–5

ISBN: 0-7424-2736-6

1 2 3 4 5 6 7 8 9 10 MAZ 10 09 08 07 06 05 04

Contents

Using Media in the Classroom

Learn to Use the News

Why Use Media in the Classroom?

Media is a fantastic tool to enhance your classroom lessons. It's inexpensive—often even free. It's the way to keep lessons current in our ever-changing world. And since your students are bombarded by media messages every day, they need your help and guidance in sorting out and understanding the news. Our goal in this guide is to help you teach your students how to evaluate and use the media to become independent readers, critical thinkers, and informed citizens. And we want to offer background and ideas to make your job just a little easier.

You'll find plenty of talking points in each chapter of this book, as well as opinions from working journalists, teachers, and media experts. You'll also find reproducible work sheets to use with your students with various units on media.

Don't be afraid to use the news. Newspapers, magazines, television reports, and media Web sites will only strengthen your lessons in each subject area, and your students will be better able to explore and understand the world around them once they know how to use the news media, too.

"The way I look at it, we really are functioning in an environment of almost information overload," says Dr. Kim Piper-Aiken, a professor at Michigan State University's school of journalism.

What can you as a teacher do with that overload? Plug right into it and help your students learn to use the news as informed consumers.

Elementary school is a perfect time to start.

Says Piper-Aiken, "At the university level, we still encounter students who are not media literate. I think we need to start in elementary and middle school and get students to engage in news consumption, whether it's newspapers, radio, or television."

Another reason to use media is that it reaches all kinds of learners, including those who need lessons beyond the textbook. Piper-Aiken points out that studies have shown that "only a small percentage of students learn effectively through the traditional textbook format." She feels strongly that teachers should reach out to all kinds of learners, including those who think visually or are tactile—hands-on—learners.

A choice of media allows students to explore a subject independently and in greater depth, in ways that match their learning styles. Says Piper-Aiken, "We know now to use other sources of material to reach all kinds of learners."

You'll want to teach your students how to navigate through a wide variety of news sources, showing them how to use newspaper and magazine indexes and tables of contents, just as you would teach them how to navigate Web sites on the Internet. By integrating materials from the media into your daily lessons, you'll enhance the subject matter.

Media literacy needn't be a separate subject to teach. Once your students have learned the basics of using media, they'll be ready to use it for help in social studies, math, geography, science, and language arts lessons. And don't forget about international media. It's a passport to greater global understanding. Use the news and you'll be using materials across your curriculum that engage students, making them better readers, writers, and thinkers. ☉

Lesson Notes and Activity Materials

- Scissors for cutting out articles
- Recent news magazines such as *Time, Newsweek, Time for Kids*, or others suitable for your students
- Internet access for individual or group work
- The activity "News and You" (p. 7) is a good weekend assignment so students have enough time to poll the number of people required.

Expert Opinion

Patricia Orlowitz, a public information officer with U.S. Aid for International Development (USAID) in Kosovo, encourages teachers to go global. Orlowitz places a high value on sharing a global perspective with students and reminds teachers that with the Internet and cable television, international print media is easier than ever to access. It's a small world, after all. The media makes sense for any teacher who wants to take his or her students around the world, getting a global perspective on issues in the news and a great grasp of geography.

Living overseas, what differences do you see between international news and American news coverage?

Here in Kosovo—and just a few months ago, in Moldova—it's a clear difference between what is reported on CNN International or CNN America (there's a big difference between those two), but you'll see an even bigger difference when you watch EuroNews or DeutschWeil (DW TV, the German public/state broadcaster). It's clear just in watching the "sport" (not called sports)—I see football from all the countries (European football, that is), curling championships in Switzerland, Tour de France cycling (live—that's big news), even cricket. But I can't think

of a time when I've heard American football—except the Super Bowl—get more than a one-line mention of the winner, and baseball, never. The difference in news is the same as in sport—I see different stories if I switch from CNN over to DW TV, and when it is the same story, it is presented with a different perspective, with different speakers, different experts analyzing it. Sometimes it is hard to believe you are seeing the same issue reported on. And I find European reporting seems to have less of the personality of the broadcasters than U.S. TV—so I think I am focusing more on the story than the presenter.

You've said that you—and other Americans overseas—really rely on the Internet to keep in touch. What are some of your favorite reliable sources?

Almost every morning, for about thirty minutes, I do a quick read of the headlines in the *New York Times* (especially the international news section and opinion-editorial page), BBC Worldwide, the Kosovo newspapers, Serbian newspapers, and Radio Free Europe news. This is a quick skim—and I might e-mail articles to myself to read later. And I listen to, watch, or access online CNN, Fox News, and NPR.

When I'm writing speeches, I use numerous sites, some for inspiration and ideas and some for research. For

research, I rely on Google as a search engine, but I also use Yahoo, especially Yahoo countries. I use Merriam-Webster's Word-of-the-Day—just to keep up on my English—it's easy to let my vocabulary slip as I study Albanian (or any foreign language), and I like the word history in this online dictionary. It

I miss reading "real" paper newspapers.

shows the international influence on the English language.

But I miss reading "real" paper newspapers. By using the Internet for news, I often go straight to the sections I need—like international news. That means I miss a lot of other articles. But when I held a newspaper in my hand and turned pages, my eye would be caught by interesting headlines, quotes, photos, a paragraph here or there—and often, it might be an article that, based just on the headline (all I see on the Internet) I wouldn't have read. But when I read one of those articles, I learn something—maybe it teaches me something about the world, about the relationship between things—or even something personally useful like a health tip. And I miss the advertising—it was more than seeing the prices or the sales—but seeing what might be the styles or what things are being promoted, like how common cell phones are—the first time I realized mobile phones were going to be big was by noticing the increase in ads and companies offering mobile phone services.☺

　　　　　5　　　　　0-7424-2736-6 *Using Media in the Classroom*

Sites and Sources

Many media outlets have Web sites where your students can easily check out what someone a thousand miles away is reading. Thanks to the Internet, students can travel abroad and catch up with foreign opinions, news, and cultures on newspaper and television Web sites such as the BBC, the *International Herald Tribune*, and CNN World News. Here are some of Orlowitz's favorites and our recommendations. You will want to explore many more. Remember to check Web sites before you use them with students, because some Web sites have very similar names to sites with content that is not appropriate for children. The Web sites listed in this book were current as this guide went to press. (For more on the Internet, see unit 5.)☉

www.nytimes.com .... the *New York Times* Web site

www.xe.com/ucc/ .... a Web site that shows currency conversions

www.m-w.com .... the *Merriam-Webster Dictionary* site

www.cnn.com .... the Web site of the twenty-four-hour cable news channel CNN

www.medialit.org .... the Web site for the Center for Media Literacy, a nonprofit group providing resources on the use of media and media literacy

www.iht.com .... the Web site of the *International Herald Tribune* newspaper

www.news.bbc.co.uk/cbbc......... the Web site for news from the British Broadcasting Corporation

www.thetimes.com..................... the Web site of the *Times* (London)

www.smh.com.au....................... the Web site of the *Sydney Morning Herald* newspaper in Australia

News and You

Where do you get your news?

Poll five people (family or friends) on how they get their news. Use the chart below to record your answers. Each person must select just one type of media. Poll information will be graphed in class.

My most important source of information is:

	newspaper	television	magazines	Internet	radio
person 1					
person 2					
person 3					
person 4					
person 5					

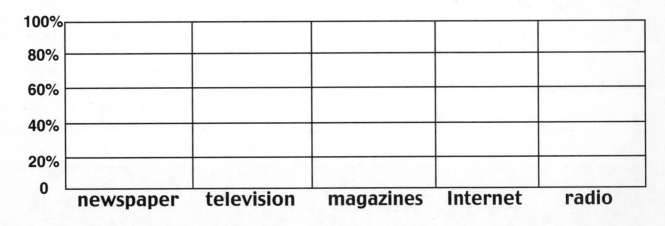

Name_____ Date _____

Learn to Use the Newspaper

Look at the first section of a newspaper and answer the following questions.

Name of newspaper

_____

Date _____

1. How many stories are on the front page?

_____

2. Find the index on the front page. Find the following sections or departments in the paper. Usually, newspapers assign letters to sections, as well as page numbers.

Where are the local-news pages?

_____

Where are the features?

_____

Where are the comics?

_____

Where is the opinion/editorial page?

_____

On what page is the movie guide?

_____

On what page is the weather?

_____

3. Find an interesting story and clip it out of the paper.

Story headline

_____

Is the reporter named? If so, what's the name?

_____

Write three facts in the story that caught your interest.

_____

_____

_____

_____

_____

Attach the story to this work sheet. On the clipping, write the name of the paper (you can abbreviate), the date of the paper, and the section and page number where you found the story.

Most newspapers have Web sites. Try to find the address of this newspaper's Web site. It's usually on the front page.

Write it here.

_____

Name_____   Date _____

Know Your Neighbors

Did you know you can read lots of newspapers from other countries on the Internet? For example, you can find out what's going on with our neighbor to the north, Canada. Visit the Web site of one of Canada's big newspapers, the *Globe and Mail*, at *www.globeandmail.com*, and answer the following questions about the news of the day in Canada.

Time you went to the Web site

_____

Main headline/news story

_____

_____

Top sports story of the day

_____

_____

Today's weather report

_____

How does the online news from Canada compare with news in your hometown newspaper? Are the same stories reported?

_____

_____

_____

What is different?

_____

_____

_____

Name_____ Date_____

Learn to Use a News Magazine

Select a news magazine and use it to answer the following questions.

Name of magazine

_____

Date of issue

_____

1. What is the cover story?

_____

2. On what page is the table of contents?

_____

3. List three departments, or sections, in the magazine.

_____

_____

_____

4. Find a story that interests you. Clip the story and attach it to this work sheet.

Name of story/headline _____

_____

Writer _____

List three facts you learned from the story.

_____

_____

_____

5. Most magazines have Web sites. The Web sites are listed in the magazines, sometimes even on the cover. Does this magazine have a Web site? If so, what is the address?

_____

Name_____   Date_____

Tune In to News

Watch a nightly newscast and answer the following questions as you watch and right after you watch.

Date and time of newscast

_____

Channel and network

_____

Name of main newscaster

_____

1. The top story is the first story in the newscast. What was the top story?

_____

2. What story was the most interesting to you?

_____

3. Write three facts from this story.

_____

_____

_____

4. Many networks and TV stations have a Web site. It is usually mentioned near the end of the program. Try to watch for it. Write the Web site address.

_____

_____

Name_____   Date _____

Find News Online

With your teacher's help, go to a news Web site—one that is connected to a newspaper, to a magazine, or to a TV network. When you get to the home page, answer the following questions about the news stories you find. You may have to follow links to find some of the stories.

1. Name a story you see on the main page. Write a fact from this story.

_____

_____

_____

2. Find the sports site and write a fact from a sports story.

_____

_____

_____

3. Find a story about entertainment—either music, movies, or TV. Write a fact from the story.

_____

_____

_____

4. Many Web sites have links to other Web sites. Write down one other Web site that is linked to this news site.

_____

_____

_____

How the Media Works

Get to Know the Media

Although children are savvy to technology, many are not media savvy. They've grown up knowing how to click a mouse from an early age, and many can find their way around the Internet searching for homework answers, but can they recognize a credible news source online?

And, thanks to cable, they've grown up with more choices in television than we ever could have imagined when we were growing up. But can they tell the difference between an entertainment show with a newsy format and the nightly network news? Are both programs reliable news sources?

Fortunately for children, the media is paying attention to them as an important audience. Many newspapers are trying to reach young readers with special features or sections just for them, and of course, there are piles of magazines aimed at young readers. Teachers can be reassured that the constant competition will benefit students, at least where youth products are concerned.

So where should students get their news? And how can you get your students to think critically about the media messages they encounter?

Michigan school teacher Barb Samra thinks media is an excellent way to generate discussion in her classroom in her Roseville middle school. Even in middle school, though, she finds she needs to teach her students how to read a newspaper much more than to teach them how to navigate with a computer mouse.

every major city. The "penny papers" were so named because they were sold for just one cent, so many readers had access to the news.

Newspapers, even at fifty cents a copy, are still a great bargain, and with the exception of the news sites on the Internet, the most up-to-date and complete

Newspapers, even at fifty cents a copy, are still a great bargain.

Know Your Newspaper

We're starting with newspapers—the oldest form of information gathering. Some textbooks date the idea of a newspaper to early journals in China fifteen hundred years ago. In America, the first newspaper published was in 1690 in Boston. One of the most famous early journalists was Benjamin Franklin. Franklin first was apprenticed to his brother and was so eager to be published that he wrote letters to the editor under another name. Later, of course, he became not only a leading diplomat but also a successful publisher.

By the late 1800s, inexpensive newspapers were sprouting up in

source of information to read. (Teachers can get discounts on newspapers for the classroom through a program called Newspaper in Education. Many newspapers across the country have this program and are happy to encourage young readers to use the newspaper.) Even adults who tune in daily to TV news often reach for a newspaper when big news happens or to follow local sports and school news.

How Does News Work?

At a newspaper, it's the newsroom that determines what you'll read each day. But the word *newsroom* doesn't refer to one

(continued on page 14)

Lesson Notes and Activity Materials

Provide recent issues of magazines and daily newspapers, particularly editorials and opinion articles, including letters to the editor and book and movie reviews. Find articles that include interviews. Students will also need articles with action verbs—sports articles may be especially useful here.

0-7424-2736-6 *Using Media in the Classroom*

mysterious room or one department. It refers to the staff that gathers, writes, and edits all sections of the paper, separate from the business side that handles delivery and advertising.

At a daily newspaper, usually a half-dozen departments are divided into areas of coverage, including local, national, and world news, sports, entertainment, business, and food or home news. The larger the newspaper, the more departments it will likely have. There also is a photography department and an art or graphics staff. In each department are editors and writers. The writer, or reporter, is often assigned a beat, a specific area or subject to cover. A sportswriter might be on the basketball beat; a news reporter might cover schools and education issues.

Here's how the structure of a newspaper works on an average day. We'll start with the local news coverage, which often happens on a daily-assignment basis.

Early in the day, reporters are assigned stories to cover. Some reporters may head out to cover the police department; others may check in on local government. Some will be assigned to cover "breaking" news—unplanned events happening that day, such as a fire or a weather-related story. Some stories are planned, including meetings such as city council, school board, or planning commission. Events such as speakers or important visitors to a community are newsworthy, as well.

Editors gather in the morning to review the day's "budget"— meaning, in this case, what stories are happening or planned. For a morning newspaper, writers will be working on stories until mid-afternoon. Then their editors review the stories and send them to the copy desk, where they are again edited for accuracy and grammar, as well as general readability. A page designer works with the editors on where and how the story will be displayed. If there is a photo involved, a photo editor is also part of the process.

By early evening, the top editors gather to decide what stories merit the front page. These are the newsiest and most timely stories. The front page is usually a mix of stories, unless one huge news event dominates.

In other forms of media, such as TV and radio, the news-gathering process is much the same. Even weekly magazines follow this process but with a weekly deadline. Decisions on covering the news are made and executed by a team of people. What you see in the paper or on TV is the result of that process.

The selection and "play" of each story is shaped by the view of the decision makers at each media organization. That's important for your students to know so they can realize that even the most fair-minded media has points in the production where some stories are selected and other stories are not printed or emphasized. However, for the most part, journalists today strive to be fair.

"Everyone has biases. I have biases, but the question is not whether I have biases. The question is, is the story handled professionally and balanced?" says Leonard Poger, a retired community newspaper editor who covered metropolitan Detroit for more than forty years. Poger, who covered thousands of local government and school board meetings during his career, says it's fine for reporters and editors to have opinions—everyone does— but your readers shouldn't feel like you're trying to push one topic or issue over another. Poger says an overwhelming percentage of reporters and editors are very professional, well balanced, and fair. He advises teachers to talk about what they see in the news and to discuss issues of fairness with students.

Dr. Kim Piper-Aiken, professor at Michigan State University's school of journalism, echoes Poger's words when she says, "I want teachers to help students understand that reporters are professional. They try as hard as they can—with the exception of people who are unethical, and there are going to be some people in every profession that are unethical.... The daily reporter tries very hard to be fair and balanced and tries to give as many sides to the story as possible.

"The other myth we need to dispel is that there are two sides to every story. There are probably dozens of angles to every story, to every news topic we have."

The other myth we need to dispel is that there are two sides to every story.

How TV News Works

The process of gathering news for a television newscast works much the same as in daily print media.

However, Kevin Roseborough, an executive producer at the Fox station in Detroit and a former

(continued on page 15)

newspaper journalist, sees the faster pace of TV as the main difference. Newspapers come out just once a day, but a station in a large viewing area has several newscasts throughout the day.

Here's how Roseborough describes a typical day. Much like newspapers, the staff begins with

newscast you see is the result of many people's work—from the first interviews to what the producers select and how much air time the story is given. A big investigative story could be five or six minutes long, but an average story often airs for ninety seconds—or even less.

start is the newspaper opinion or editorial pages, where there are not only the unsigned editorials from the newspaper staff but a mix of columnists and letters to the editor. Here, opinion is the name of the game. Magazines also usually carry letters from readers and opinion pieces.

News coverage is supposed to be straightforward and free of opinion.

a morning news meeting in which they discuss what happened the day before, what is on the schedule for the day, and what people have heard that morning on radio or read in the newspaper. News leads and ideas are discussed as well.

Roseborough says, "From there, we develop a plan beginning with the next show and deploy our reporters and their camera person (to the assignment). Some stories are shot and physically returned to the station for editing and broadcast. Others are shot (taped), then edited in one of the big 'live' trucks you see all painted up with station logos and transmitted back to the station via microwave for broadcast.

"When a reporter does a live shot, the truck feeds the signal back to the station for broadcast."

Just like newspapers, a TV news show has an assignment desk. Producers are in charge of checking stories and deciding when a reporter should do a full story and how the story should be presented. Should a news anchor read the story? Or should someone be interviewed on camera?

Producers have writers who help pull the newscast together, once the show is set. Then show directors, says Roseborough, coordinate the camera angles and when graphics are used. The

Now that you're more familiar with the behind-the-scenes workings of both television and newspaper newsrooms, you can convey this information to your students. To give them a better understanding of what editors and writers do, use some of the work sheets included in this section (pp. 17–28).

A Matter of Opinion

For the most part, news coverage is supposed to be straightforward and free of opinion. However, there are some places where opinions are welcome and, indeed, expected. And these days, there is no shortage of opinion. From liberal to conservative, and every viewpoint in between, there are plenty of folks taking a stand in print, on TV, and definitely on the radio.

Opinion pieces are great ways to hone students' critical thinking when comparing and contrasting voices in the media. In the newspaper and in magazines, the main place to find opinions is on the editorial page or in the letters section. However, your students can find columnists in every section of the paper. Especially in big-city newspapers, columnists write about sports, lifestyle, and advice. Another place to look for opinion is in reviews of movies, television, and music.

Of course, the clear place to

Talk news shows on TV frequently feature commentary pieces or panel discussions that offer particular points of view. Radio shows have similar formats. The Internet, of course, is loaded with opinions from media Web sites as well as from individuals who make an enterprise of speaking out in cyberspace.

Editorial opinions don't show up only in print media. Commentators like Bill O'Reilly and Rush Limbaugh are not news reporters. They express opinions for particular points of view. "People don't really understand that as clearly as they do in newspapers," points out Piper-Aiken. Newspapers clearly define places and spaces for news reporting and opinion columns and editorials. In television, those lines are not always so clear, especially in some of the formatted news talk shows. Teachers need to explain the difference in news where there is a presumption of fairness and objectivity, which would be true on any of the main network newscasts, and in so-called news where people are trying to engage people's opinions about issues. She urges teachers to help students clearly distinguish between factual presentations of material as opposed to shows that are showcases for opinions based on the news.

It's hard, initially, for students in grades four and five to recognize the difference between straightforward facts and opinion pieces. Use the work sheets included (pp. 17–28) to help them sharpen their skills and become (continued on page 16)

familiar with opinion pieces. This is a great place to write letters to the editor from your class. (You'll find a letter work sheet included in this section; see p. 19). Have your students write the letters and ask parent volunteers to neatly type the letters so you can submit a package to your local newspaper. Many newspapers welcome occasional letters from young readers. There also is a Newspaper in Education week in early March each year, and often newspapers offer space on the editorial page that week for young readers.

We hope this behind-the-scenes look at TV and newspapers gives you a better understanding to pass on to your students. To give them a firsthand look at media, consider a field trip to your local television station or community newspaper. Many media outlets are willing to give tours or have speakers from their staffs visit schools. ⏰

Sites and Sources

www.newspapers.com .... a source for teachers to find U.S. or international newspaper addresses. It's also a great place to find special sites related to newspaper areas of coverage: movies, weather, business, and so on.

www.world-newspapers.com .... a source for everyone. It allows you to click on a region of the world or country and then click on a newspaper (in English) Web site.

http://people-press.org .... the Web site of the Pew Research Center for the People and the Press, sponsored by the Pew Charitable Trusts. This site offers research on the media, including polls that indicate how closely the public follows major news stories. The site also is a good information research center on a variety of media projects.

www.yahooligans.com .... the Web site on Yahoo for children. You'll find categories of interest on any topic, including media.

Name_____   Date _____

Fact or Opinion?

Do you know about "loaded" words? Opinions can be written in other pieces that are not on the opinion page, including music and movie reviews and profiles. Look for words that express the writer's point of view and for descriptive words that create a certain image. For example, read the paragraph below and look for loaded words that communicate the writer's opinion.

Actress Starr Bright stomped off the movie set, whining that the judging in the audition was unfair, even though she clearly wasn't fit for the part. Bright lost the part to competitor Sunny Sweet, who is a much better actress and who was graciously making her way to the dressing room as Bright complained.

Words like "whine" give you an image of a complaining person. Who's to say Bright "stomped" off? and how was Sunny "gracious" in her walk? Who decided that Sunny is a better actress? Can you see that the example is loaded with opinion? Pick a newspaper or magazine story and make a list of loaded words that express opinion.

Name and date of magazine or newspaper

_____

Title of article

_____

Loaded words

_____   _____

_____   _____

_____   _____

_____   _____

_____   _____

_____   _____

0-7424-2736-6 *Using Media in the Classroom*

Name_____ Date _____

Compare and Contrast

Read the two paragraphs. Use the questions that follow to contrast the writers' views.

You Should Not Keep a Lost Kitten

It is not a good idea to keep a lost kitten. You should not keep it because it may belong to someone else. Besides, you do not know how to care for a kitten. Finally, a kitten might make the whole house smell bad.

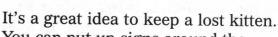

You Should Keep a Lost Kitten

It's a great idea to keep a lost kitten. You can put up signs around the neighborhood to see if the kitten belongs to someone. If you do not know how to care for a kitten, you can go to a pet store and ask for advice, you can read a book, or you can go to a veterinarian. If the kitten smells up the house, you can put a litter box in the basement or other out-of-the-way place and clean it every day to get rid of the odors.

1. The writers disagree about

_____

2. One opinion is _____

_____

3. A different opinion is _____

_____

Notice how the second writer answers the reasons given by the first writer. Can you think of any other reasons for or against keeping a lost kitten? Write them here.

_____

_____

_____

_____

4. Work with a partner. From the list of topics below, together choose one for you both to write about—one should write reasons to support the opinion, the other should write reasons against the opinion. You can talk to each other about your reasons.

Fourth graders shouldn't go on the biggest slide. Only fifth graders should.

_____ is a good movie (choose a movie you have both seen).

_____ is a good story (choose one you have both read).

Students in our school have too much homework.

Our lunch period is too short.

Students should wear uniforms to school.

Name_____ Date_____

Letter to the Editor

Your teacher has shown you opinion pieces from the editorial page of the newspaper. You've also been studying events in the news. After reading these pieces, write a letter on a subject you care about. Use the space below to organize your thoughts and write a practice letter.

Dear Editor,

I read about

I am concerned that

Here is my idea to help with this problem

Sincerely,

Your Name

School

0-7424-2736-6 *Using Media in the Classroom*

Name _____ Date _____

You're the Reviewer

Entertainment reviews always express an opinion. Use this work sheet to takes notes as you watch a TV show. Afterward, write a review of the show. Many reviews use stars to show how good a show is. Give your show a star rating: 4 stars for great, 3 stars for good, 2 stars for boring, and 1 star for so bad I turned it off.

Show name _____

Network or channel _____

Main character _____

What happened _____

Did it make you laugh? _____

What did you like? _____

What did you dislike? _____

Would you recommend this show to a friend? _____

Fill in the number of stars you would give this show.

☆ ☆ ☆ ☆

Did any of your classmates watch the show? _____ Compare opinions with them.

_____

_____

I Disagree

Find a review you disagree with on a book, movie, music release, or video game. Answer the questions below first. Then, on another paper, write an editorial for a newspaper telling why you disagree with the reviewer's opinion. Include the reasons why you like or dislike the product. Be sure to attach the original review to your paper.

1. Summarize the reviewer's opinion in one sentence.

_____

_____.

2. List the reasons the reviewer gives in support of her or his opinion.

_____

_____

_____

3. What is the reviewer's strongest reason in support of the opinion?

_____

_____

_____

4. Do you think that reason is a good one? Why or why not?

_____

_____

5. What is the reviewer's second strongest reason?

_____

6. Do you think that reason is a good one? Why or why not?

_____

7. Summarize your opinion about the matter.

_____

8. List reasons in support of your opinion.

_____

9. What is your strongest reason that supports your opinion? (When you start writing your editorial, you may want to present that reason first.)

_____

_____

Be a Sports Columnist

Sportswriters try to cover games fairly. But if they write opinion columns, they are allowed to give their thoughts on games or events. Watch your favorite college or professional team play on TV. In the space below, take notes. On the back of this page, write an opinion of the game—either how the team played, how they were coached, or both. Be sure to back up your opinion with some examples from your notes.

Sport

_____

Teams playing

_____

_____

Do you have a favorite of the two teams?

_____

If so, which team?

_____

As you watch, notice decisions coaches or players make. Decide if each was a good decision or a bad decision.

_____

_____

_____

_____

_____

_____

Ask the Right Questions

Journalists learn the 5 Ws and 1 H—a group of questions that helps them gather the facts on any story. The letters stand for Who, Where, What, When, Why, and How. Use this work sheet to answer the 5 Ws and 1 H about a story you read in the newspaper. Attach the story to the work sheet when you finish.

Headline of story

_____

Name of magazine/newspaper and date of publication

_____

Who is the story about?

_____

Where does the story take place?

_____

What happened?

_____

_____

When did it happen?

_____

Why did it happen?

_____

_____

_____

How did it happen?

_____

_____

_____

_____

_____

_____

_____

_____

_____

Name_____ Date _____

Where's the Action?

Newspapers and magazines are full of colorful writing. Writers try to choose verbs that are especially vivid. Use a highlighter to mark action verbs in an article from a newspaper or magazine. Write the verbs below, and write a new sentence using each verb. Attach the story to this work sheet.

Verb	Sentence
_____	_____
_____	_____
_____	_____
_____	_____
_____	_____
_____	_____
_____	_____
_____	_____
_____	_____

Name_____   Date _____

Headlines and Deadlines

The headline is the title of a news or a feature story. A headline should sum up the main point and make you want to read the story. Select a headline from today's newspaper. Cut it out and paste it in the space below.

Paste your headline here.

```



```

1. What does the headline tell you is the main point of the story?

_____

_____

_____

2. Now try writing a few new headlines for the same story.

_____

_____

_____

Where in the World?

Each newspaper story from a location outside your newspaper's hometown usually carries a *dateline*—a line at the beginning that names the city the reporter is writing from. (Originally the date was included with the location. That's why it's called a *dateline*.) Look at a national or world page in your newspaper and find five different datelines. Then find the cities on a map and write what country and continent each is in. Why is this city making news?

	City	Country	Continent	News
1.				
2.				
3.				
4.				
5.				

Name_____ Date _____

The Interview

Television, magazines, and newspapers all cover interesting people. A reporter interviews a person to get information that readers or viewers don't know. Your teacher will assign you to interview someone in your class. Use some or all of the questions below to get started. Think of more questions of your own if you want to. After the interview, write a paragraph on another paper telling about the person you interviewed.

Name of person interviewed _____

1. What is the thing you do best?

   _____

2. Who is your favorite hero?

   _____

   Why is she or he your favorite?

   _____

3. What are your ideas about what you might want to be when you grow up?

   _____

4. What chores do you have to do at home?

   _____

5. Do you have any pets? If so, tell me about them.

   _____

   _____

6. Do you have sisters or brothers? If so, what activities do you do together? If not, what would you like to do with brothers and sisters if you had them?

   _____

   _____

7. Have you traveled any place you'd like to tell about?

   _____

Name_____   Date_____

Same Day, Different News?

Your assignment is to compare and contrast a TV newscast with the front-page news of a daily newspaper. First, get the daily newspaper and make a list of the front-page headlines. Then, to do your comparison, watch the 6 P.M. nightly news and, using the space below, write down the main stories (this can include weather and sports stories). What stories are the same? What stories are different?

Today's Big Stories

Newspaper   **TV**

1. _____   _____

2. _____   _____

3. _____   _____

4. _____   _____

5. _____   _____

6. _____   _____

Prepare for Politics

Every four years, social studies lessons come alive as the nation elects a president. Election years are an especially exciting time in the news media as reporters track the campaigns. But congressional, state, and local elections—even in nonpresidential election years—are ideal for students to see democracy in action.

Newspapers, magazines, and television—with daily updates on issues, candidates, and parties—are vital teaching tools. It's easy to assign students news shows to watch but even handier to clip articles from newspapers and magazines to track issues. The Internet also has good Web sites attached to every major newspaper and news magazine that give diverse perspectives.

Here are some ideas for lessons planned around political coverage. We're shaping these activities around a presidential election, but they can be adapted for congressional, gubernatorial, and even mayoral elections, as well.

The Campaign Trail

Nine months to a year ahead of the election, candidates are in the media daily as they make a case for being nominated by their parties for president. This is a great time to assign your class, in groups, to research each candidate and present information that can later help your class vote in a mock election.

The Iowa caucuses and the New Hampshire primary are the first tests for presidential candidates. When you start studying the campaign, it's a good opportunity to bring geography into the les-

Every four years, social studies lessons come alive.

sons. Your students will be able to see how their candidates did in each state's early nominating votes. The newspaper from your hometown will be covering the visits to your state. Have students clip daily articles and highlight the positions candidates express. Then, using the Internet and news magazines, they can track how the candidates are doing in other states.

The network TV shows usually include coverage of the campaign trail on the evening newscast, as do the Sunday morning news talk shows. You may want to assign students to watch some of those shows, along with checking the networks' Web sites. At the end of this chapter, check out our list of safe, reliable resources that explain and cover the political process.

Map the Campaign

Your students can follow the campaign trail in class and learn geography in the process. Post a large U.S. map on a bulletin board (or a state map if the election is a state race). Use different color pushpins for different candidates.

Using a daily newspaper or news media Web site, have students track the stops of each candidate. The stories in newspapers and magazines will often carry datelines at the start of the story to show where the candidate is. By the end of the campaign, your map should show what states (or regions of your state) the candidates think are key to winning votes. In national election years, chances are you'll see a big cluster of pushpins in states like Michigan, New York, and California.

Survey Your School

Opinion polls are a huge part of media coverage. Networks, newspapers, and magazines regularly commission polling companies to gauge the opinions and support of voters on a variety of issues and, in an election year,

(continued on page 30)

Lesson Notes and Activity Materials

Provide current newspapers and news magazines for students to research candidates.

the support for candidates. Have your classroom develop a poll and poll each class and, if time, the entire school.

Fact or Opinion?

Political coverage is a great place to have students use their critical-thinking skills. On television and in the print media, the press attempts to offer unbiased coverage in news stories, saving opinion pieces for commentators, columnists, and editorial writers. You can collect samples of stories and samples of opinion pieces. Read some aloud to your students and see if your class can tell the difference between opinion pieces and straight news. Discuss the differences. You can also use politics as a way to compare how the press differs in reporting on candidates. Compare, for example, a *Wall Street Journal* report of a candidate's speech with one in

Talk about formats of debates. In most presidential debates, journalists ask questions and candidates are given two minutes (or a certain time limit) to answer. Both or all of the candidates respond to the same question. Another format uses the single moderator: One person poses the questions. In the town meeting style of debate, people from the audience get to ask questions. Even if students can't stay up late enough to see the debates on TV, you can follow the debates in the newspaper the next day.

Once you've educated students on debate processes, you can stage a classroom debate. Start by clipping out newspaper and magazine articles on the major issues (where do candidates stand on education, the environment, and health care?). Create a file folder with information on each candidate. Then, after you've created a

time keepers. Each candidate should have a chance to respond to each question.

Cast Your Votes

A week or two before the real election is the ideal time to have a mock election in your classroom. Your students have studied the candidates and the issues, and now they're ready to vote. Make a simple ballot and a ballot box. Voting should be private. Try to create a voting booth by using a large appliance box or use pieces of cardboard to create a privacy barrier around a desk. You might even check with your local League of Women Voters or city hall to see if either would set up devices for a mock election. Some towns will bring equipment to a school event because they want to encourage future voters.

On television and in the print media, the press attempts to offer unbiased coverage in news stories.

---

your local newspaper. Your students may find differences in what is stressed in each story. Although newspapers strive to be fair and balanced, they have different audiences and will look at key issues in different ways.

Again, this is an excellent opportunity to discuss what students reading and how reading a wide variety of sources will help make students most informed.

The Great Debate

Debates are a great opportunity for voters to see where the candidates stand on the issues. Help your students understand the debate process ahead of time.

file for each candidate, divide the class into three groups, one representing the Democratic candidate, one representing the Republican candidate, and a third representing an independent candidate or the leading alternative candidate. Each group will choose one person to play its candidate. You can be the moderator of the debate.

For the debate, assign students new jobs. Some will remain party representatives and stay with the candidate as advisors to help him or her answer the questions in the debate. Another group of students will become journalists asking questions or reporters covering the debate. Some students can be

Math Matters

Once the vote is in, you'll want to count and graph the results. There's nothing like a vote count to make math exciting. You can even do a mock exit poll and try to graph the results ahead of the final tally. Graph the results according to gender and by grade. See if the exit poll results match the real vote results.

(continued on page 31)

After the Election

When a new president takes office, journalists often refer to the honeymoon period when covering the president's first days on the job. Sometimes that will be a month, sometimes only a few days if a news crisis develops. During the honeymoon period, the president has lots of support from the public and the press holds back on criticism, waiting until the new leader settles into the job. Have your students evaluate news coverage during a president's first weeks in office and see if they agree that the president is treated differently than usual. ☉

Sites and Sources

You can send your students to these helpful sites to track our political process.

www.kidsvotingusa.org	the Web site of the nonprofit group Kids Voting USA, which gives political information plus ways students can get involved in mock elections. Kids Voting sponsors its elections with partners.
www.lwv.org	League of Women Voters—a good site for background for teachers to shape discussions and talking points on the voting process and on candidates.
www.americanpresident.org	history and facts on our presidents, from the University of Virginia's Miller Center for Public Affairs
www.vote-smart.org	the Web site of Project Vote Smart, a nonprofit group that aims to inform voters without bias on elected officials, issues, and candidates. This site is easy to use and can give teachers plenty of background material in shaping lessons.
www.whitehouse.gov/kids/	the official White House site for children
www.newseum.org	the Web site of the Newseum in the Washington, D.C., metro area that shows how newspapers and media work and especially focuses on politics and freedom of the press

Know the Candidates

Get to know the candidates. Using newspapers, magazines, television, and the Internet, gather basic biographical facts about a candidate running for office.

Candidate's name _____

Running for (office) _____

Political party _____

Current hometown _____

Age and birthplace _____

Family _____

Where did the candidate go to high school and college?

_____

What kind of work does she or he do?

_____

Fun facts (pets, favorite music or sports, favorite books, hobbies)

_____

What are some things the candidate says she or he will do if elected?

_____

_____

_____

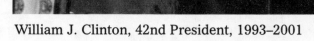

William J. Clinton, 42nd President, 1993–2001

Name_____ Date _____

Political Fact or Opinion?

Can you separate fact from opinion? Clip out an article from a newspaper or a magazine about a candidate or about someone in an elected office. Then find three facts from the story. Are there any opinion statements? Fill out the sheet below.

Fact

1. _____

2. _____

3. _____

Opinion

_____

_____

_____

_____

_____

_____

_____

_____

_____

_____

Political Cartooning

1. What point is the artist making in this cartoon?

   _____

   _____

   _____

2. Try your hand at political cartooning. On another piece of paper, create a cartoon about a political leader and something he or she has done. Need ideas to get started? Turn to the editorial page of your newspaper or the cartoon page in your favorite news magazine.

Name_____   Date _____

Playground Poll

Polls are a popular way for newspapers, magazines, and TV networks to gather opinions. Use this work sheet for a poll on recess rules. Poll five students and total the results. After the poll is finished, share the results in class. Your teacher will help you graph the results.

1. Do students get enough recess time?

Person 1	yes	no
Person 2	yes	no
Person 3	yes	no
Person 4	yes	no
Person 5	yes	no

2. Should students be allowed to play group sports during recess?

Person 1	yes	no
Person 2	yes	no
Person 3	yes	no
Person 4	yes	no
Person 5	yes	no

3. Does our school need more playground and sports equipment?

Person 1	yes	no
Person 2	yes	no
Person 3	yes	no
Person 4	yes	no
Person 5	yes	no

Party Animals

Around election time, you see a lot of elephants and donkeys. The elephant is a symbol of the Republican Party, and the donkey is a symbol of the Democratic Party. If you were choosing a symbol for a new political party, what animal symbol would you use and why? Draw your party animal in the space below.

Animal _____

1. Why I chose this animal _____

_____

_____

_____

2. Draw a picture of your animal.

3. Think of a name for your new party. _____

4. What would be your party's platform (its principles)? _____

_____

_____

Name _____   Date _____

Political Talk

Lots of special words are used in news about politics. Some may not be familiar. First, find a definition for each word below.

Then, find the word used in a magazine or newspaper story. Write the sentence containing the word.

poll _____

_____

_____

_____

ballot _____

_____

_____

_____

incumbent _____

_____

_____

_____

front-runner _____

_____

_____

_____

platform _____

_____

_____

_____

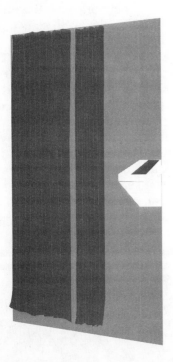

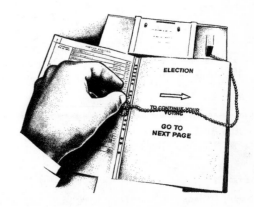

ELECTION

TO CONTINUE YOUR VOTING

GO TO NEXT PAGE

0-7424-2736-6 *Using Media in the Classroom*

Tuned In to Television

Today's students have grown up with cable, dish, and satellite TV and all the selections to fit every taste and every age. Such nonstop TV offerings can be a problem when it comes to exercise and homework, but you as a teacher can use the attraction to TV to your advantage. Your students will tune in to you when you discuss television or use the television news to help teach current events.

"Nobody does a better job visualizing the news for students, particularly with one-hour news specials and town-hall style meetings," says Ann Orr, executive director of the National Association of Broadcasters' Education Foundation. Among the strengths of TV news, says Orr, are the special in-depth broadcast reports. These reports offer news from primary sources, with journalists on locations around the world showing viewers firsthand what is happening.

Another strength of television news is its immediacy, whether hearing from world leaders in time of crisis or from ordinary citizens in faraway places or close to home. Third, in-depth news coverage can give students an easy-to-digest analysis of the news of the day.

"It's helpful and important to employ television as an edu-

Television is an immediate media and is ideal for following breaking news.

cational tool because students do spend a lot of time watching TV. It's the media that speaks to them directly...they're used to watching it and they trust it," says Orr.

In our rapidly changing world, television news is rapidly changing, too.

Michigan State's Dr. Kim Piper-Aiken compares the thirty-minute newscast of the three major networks, the choice when she was growing up, to the twenty-four-hour cable news stations like CNN, MSNBC, and Fox News today. Such constant coverage leads to overplaying and sensationalizing stories. News covers more stories on celebrities and on crime. The competition for viewers determines the content of the coverage.

The competition also means that better news shows have evolved. That's good news for young viewers as well as for adults. Networks are required to carry children's educational programming, and some networks, such as Nickelodeon and Disney, are devoted entirely to children's programming. These networks show news programs for children along with special reports

and educational entertainment.

Orr says the visual impact of television is very appealing to children. During election years, political coverage, including debates, can help your students become informed about the candidates.

There are always major stories in other subject areas, too, including science. Space missions are ideal for students to follow through television. Television is an immediate media and is ideal for following breaking news. Kevin Roseborough, an executive producer at the Fox network affiliate in Detroit, Michigan, says, "Television's strength is its ability to provide moving pictures and instantaneous coverage."

Every network puts the news on a Web site as well, so even if students can't catch a live news show, they can compare the TV report with print media's story.

Entertainment is a big part of the information presentation on TV. Your students can sharpen their critical-thinking skills by evaluating news coverage. Is it information? Is it entertainment? Does it sensationalize an event? Is it clear, or is it confusing?

(continued on page 39)

Lesson Notes and Activity Materials

Students will follow TV weather forecasts for a week, and the "TV Diary" activity suggests giving students two days to gather their data.

You can also point out to your students how TV uses graphics and music in the presentation of the news, sports, and weather. Tell your students to pay attention to the people presenting the news. There usually is a lead newscaster, called the anchor, and often a second newsreader and a weather reporter. Then there are reporters out on assignment with camera crews on the scene.

Style and presentation are very much a part of today's news coverage. You can help your students understand that just like a well-crafted ad helps sell a product, news is presented to consumers in a polished package. The networks aim to report the news and to get as many viewers as possible, just like newspapers and magazines want to get as many readers as possible. News is big business, and television is how the majority of Americans, especially young people, get their news.☉

Television satellites transmit digital information and images to individual stations through the use of microwaves.

Expert Opinion

Dr. Kim Piper-Aiken is a professor at Michigan State University's school of journalism. Piper-Aiken specializes in the study of broadcast journalism. She has worked in media, including  radio and television reporting and production. It's Piper-Aiken's business to stay informed and to study what's going on in the media.

Where do you get most of your news?

I read the *New York Times*—I get it online every day. I watch all the network (news broadcasts) as I have time. I do a lot of my analysis of television news by watching it. I also try to watch a Lansing-based broadcast of each of the stations at least once or twice a week because I have several students who are working in that market. I read the *Lansing State Journal* because I live on the outskirts of East Lansing. My son is a high school student, so I like to keep track of school issues. I already read the *State News* (MSU's student newspaper) and I'm a big NPR listener. I love "Morning Edition" and "All Things Considered" … I also watch CNN quite a bit and read a variety of news magazines.

What tips can you offer teachers in helping their students become smart media consumers?

Source variety is important. Depending on students' ages and level of sophistication, they need to look at who is being interviewed, who are the newsmakers, and try to evaluate what those news sources are. They also need to try to evaluate how credible those news sources are. Discussions of credibility are important. We need to discuss with students—what do we mean by credibility? Why are we interested in credible news sources?

When you have an environment like the Internet, where you can go on, punch something into Google or any search engine, and look up a topic you'll often be directed to a site that looks like news but can be pretty frightening in content (and not credible).

… Students need to look at where the news is coming from—is it coming from a standard news source? … I think we could do a better job of explaining credibility and having people pick and choose sources that are credible, media outlets that are credible, and even reporters that are credible. We could all do a better job of that.☉

Expert Opinion

Kevin Roseborough is an executive producer at the Fox network affiliate in Detroit and formerly a print journalist. He can readily compare print and broadcast media.

What's the biggest difference between working at a newspaper and at a television station?

I found the biggest difference between newspaper and TV news gathering is the pace. In newspapers, you have to hit a couple of deadlines a day, and there is a lot of hustling required just to make those. In television, the whole day is a deadline.... Television news people need to switch gears in an instant.

A television station routinely requires a reporter to do two stories a day and often will change assignments many times a day in reaction to breaking news stories.

While newspapers are slower to get breaking news to their readers, by having more time and space they are able to be more complete in their coverage.

What about TV? Why is it an important medium?

The ability of a television station to tap into the good heart of its community is awe-inspiring. In recent days, our station has been approached with stories on an elderly woman who needed a dangerous tree removed and a man who lost all his teeth during cancer treatment. In both cases, we did the stories and found members of the community willing to step up and remove the tree and give the man dentures for free. Another highly important facet of TV news is the use of tape in its investigations. It is amazing how quickly improper behavior can be brought to a halt when it is caught on tape and exposes misconduct that has endangered the public.⏱

Sites and Sources

www.cnn.com .... the Web site for the twenty-four-hour Cable News Network

www.msnbc.com .... the Web site for NBC's twenty-four-hour cable network

www.weather.com .... the Web site for the Weather Channel

www.kidsnewsroom.org .... a Web site developed by parents

Almost any local station in a big metropolitan market also has a Web site. You can find them by using a search engine.

Bad Stuff in the News: A Guide to Handling the Headlines, by Rabbi Marc Gellman and Monsignor Thomas Hartman (Seastar Books, 2002). You might know the authors as the "God Squad" from appearances on ABC's *Good Morning America*. The authors offer helpful ideas for explaining bad news to young people as well as tips and advice to help children feel hopeful with a "Stuff You Can Fix" section at the end of each chapter.

Name _____   Date _____

Watch the Weather

Every local news station has a weather person to give the forecasts. Weather reports are often entertaining as well as informative. Spend a week watching the weather forecast on the local nightly news.

For each weathercast you watch, use these questions to help you take notes on how the weather information is presented each day. Use a notebook or other blank paper for your notes.

Name of weather reporter

_____

Date and channel of weather report

_____

What does the weather reporter wear?

_____

What graphics (pictures) are used for the weather report?

_____

_____

_____

Besides the forecast, what other weather news did you see? (For example, if it's winter, there might be a report on a snowstorm.)

_____

_____

Did the weather report include some humor and entertaining elements? If yes, describe the humor or entertaining elements.

_____

_____

_____

0-7424-2736-6 *Using Media in the Classroom*

Name_____ Date _____

TV Diary

Where do you and your family get your TV news? Use this sheet to write down for two days what news programs everyone in your household watches. Report the results in class and graph the results on page 43.

TV News Show	Time of Broadcast	Who Watches

Make a Graph

Graph the results of the classroom poll. Show the top news shows watched by your classmates and their families. Your graph should include the name of each show and the total number of people who watch it. You could make a line graph, a bar graph, or a pictograph.

Use the Internet

If you've ever surfed your way to the wrong Web site, you know the dangers of letting your students loose on the Web.

Middle school teacher Barb Samra is much less enamored of using Internet resources now than when she first got Web access at her school. Initially, Samra felt comfortable assigning students a project and letting them use key words and search engines to track down good research. But quickly the Internet superhighway became a very congested place, and not all roads were leading to good educational material. Samra still uses the Internet but only when giving her students specific Web sites to visit, such as NASA, at *www.nasa.gov/home/index.html*, or media outlets including the Weather Channel, *www.weather.com*.

Alice Pepper, formerly a librarian and now a Web editor at the *Detroit Free Press*, says, "Using news Web sites in the classroom doesn't mean giving up the print version. While the content—news stories, comics, sports scores, reviews, entertainment guides—is similar, the differences in format make looking at newsprint and looking at a Web site unique experiences."

Schools have tried to put filters and blocks on the Internet to make it a safe place for students to navigate, but that also has

The Internet is here to stay, and it's an amazing and valuable tool for teachers.

blocked some research sites. Still, the Internet is here to stay, and it's an amazing and valuable tool for teachers, when used with discretion and with a mix of other media.

It's particularly handy in bringing resources to your students that they would otherwise have no access to. For instance, a student who wants to write about author J. K. Rowling can find an interview with Rowling published in the *Times* (London), or in Rowling's hometown newspaper in Edinburgh, Scotland. If a student wants to check out a newspaper or magazine not in the school library, he or she can check it out on the Internet.

As a teacher, of course, you'll want to continue to use all types of media to enhance your classroom lessons.

Pepper reminds teachers to choose carefully among the media.

"Newspapers, tabloids, and magazines are each aimed at specific audiences. Their Web sites also reflect diversity in what is considered newsworthy, tasteful, and entertaining."

As journalists, we love using the Internet in our reporting. It's a great shortcut to finding good primary sources and experts on everything under the sun. It also lets us contact those experts around the world who can help provide clear and on-the-scene information for all kinds of stories (newspaper budgets, like school budgets, don't allow for lots of travel). It will be exciting to see what the future will bring in the still relatively new and expanding medium. ☉

Lesson Notes and Activity Materials

- Internet access for group or individual use
- See Rules for Online Safety (p. 46).

Expert Opinion

Alice Pepper, a Web editor at the *Detroit Free Press*, started working on *freep.com*, the *Free Press* Web site, shortly after it was launched in 1996. She works throughout the day with reporters and editors to update the site with the latest local news stories.

The Internet can be a great resource for the classroom. What are some good and bad points teachers should keep in mind when using the Web?

Some advertisements appearing in print might be offensive but easily overlooked. However, on a Web page those ads blink, wiggle, and change color—getting much more attention than the print versions. (On the plus side)… students can see Web sites for newspapers and broadcast outlets from around the world. However, some foreign newspapers are controlled by the government. What might be scandalous and blasphemous in one nation is commonplace in another. Canadian newspapers cover U.S. actions with a different point of view than ours, even though the countries are so close. Understanding how journalistic standards vary from country to country can reveal more than what is in a news article alone.

Stories often contain Web links to sites with more information on a topic, a government agency, or a business. While these Web sites are verified as accurate and appropriate when the article is written, it is possible for a Web site's domain name to be purchased by another owner and turned into something unsuitable for younger audiences.

Describe how news gets on *freep.com* and, in general, how does the process work in newsrooms where a Web site is also produced?

As each story is sent through a computer network to be turned into ink-on-paper newspaper, an electronic copy of the story is sent to the *freep.com* computer. Our Web producers start at 6 P.M., as the newspaper is getting ready to go to press.

The Web producers guide each story through several different computer programs. The stories are converted into Web language—HTML—and sorted into categories—Michigan news or travel or the Red Wings or one of a few dozen other choices. The Web producers design a "home page" by choosing three main stories, selecting an important photo as the centerpiece, and writing dozens of "teases" that link to stories in *freep.com*.

Our sports home page—one of the most popular pages on the Web site—gets the same treatment.

Around 2 A.M., after the last sports story has been written and sent to the presses, the Web producers can finish *freep.com* by sending the stories, indexes, and photos to the online Web site, where everyone can see them.

You've said that the print edition and online edition can be different. What are some differences?

A few stories that appear on *freep.com* don't appear in the newspaper. We update our Web site with breaking news throughout the day. Some stories are from wire services, others are written by *Free Press* reporters. These stories might end up in tomorrow's newspaper too, but we can use *freep.com* to be as current as television and radio news broadcasts.

What advice can you give teachers on using the Internet in class?

Pick the news sites for students to explore. There is enough content to question and discuss in individual media Web sites. When students go trolling for sites, they might get lost in the Internet swamp. Since everyone can be a publisher on the Web, there is a lot out there that is not worth reading.

As a former librarian, you know how important research is. What tips can you offer teachers and students in finding credible news and research sources?

First, don't limit your research to the Web. As big as a newspaper is, it doesn't have everything. Remember that a newspaper can't put all its print content online…. There are limitations of technology, copyright, time, and resources.

Second, use Web sites of brand-name print and broadcast outlets—*Detroit Free Press, CBS News, Washington Post*, and your local or community newspaper. Avoid sites that don't name the publisher or don't have "contact us" information.

Third, organizations for professional journalists and broadcasters have their own Web sites. These may contain links to members' sites, which often (not always) indicates the linked site is reliable. ☺

Rules for Online Safety

These may seem like common sense, but it's always a good idea to be direct about what is acceptable behavior for students working on classroom projects. Tailor these rules to fit your classroom, discuss them with students, and send a copy home to parents.

1. A parent or other adult will be in the room while a student does online research.
2. Students will use only recommended "child-safe" search engines *(Yahooligans.com, ajkids.com, dicoverykids.com)*.
3. Students will not register to use any site or give their names or any personal information without a parent's okay.
4. Students will not give a parent's credit card number or any other personal information online.

Sites and Sources

www.world-newspapers.com	a source for teachers and students that allows you to click on a region of the world or on a country and then click on a newspaper (in English) Web site
www.yahooligans.com	the junior version of the Yahoo search engine, and all the sites it lists are chosen because they are deemed appropriate for young people
www.askjeeves.com	a site with links to safe and credible research and reference
www.ajkids.com	Ask Jeeves for children, with study tools such as a dictionary and a thesaurus

Find a Web Address

Many news stories in your community paper, your school newsletter, or your favorite magazines will include a Web address for the organization, person, or institution written about. Find three Web addresses and write them in the spaces below. Why are these addresses in the news?

Story 1

Headline

_____

Web address given

_____

Why was the Web address included?

_____

_____

Story 2

Headline

_____

Web address given

_____

Why was the Web address included?

_____

_____

Story 3

Headline

_____

Web address given

_____

Why was the Web address included?

_____

_____

Pay Attention to Advertising

"I'm Lovin' It"—If you can't get that catchy phrase out of your mind, then the advertising folks for McDonald's are lovin' it. That means they've done a good job getting their message to you.

Chances are there are lots of other familiar slogans and catch phrases rolling around in your brain, too. Your students know "Just do it," "Finger lickin' good," and "Have it your way"—and they can give you more slogans anytime you ask.

Advertising is a part of all the media we've been discussing—including the Internet with those annoying pop-up ads. You can't escape advertising. Logos and brands are worn by popular sports stars, so students know the names of those companies well. Even local sports stadiums surround the playing field or rink with advertisements, and often school programs have sponsorship ads from local businesses. Public television, the last holdout against advertising, features sponsors presenting their messages at the beginning or end of a show. PBS shows such as *Sesame Street* have licensed characters, toys, and games. Advertising, after all, pays the bills for media. Messages are everywhere.

Just as you teach your students to read informational articles with a critical eye, you need to fill them in on advertising so they can recognize the impact that advertising messages have on them.

Children see an amazing number of advertisements. The average young person views about forty thousand ads on TV in one year, says advertising expert Shari Graydon. Add to that number the thousands of ads they hear on the radio or view on the Internet, in magazines, and in newspapers, and you've got one staggering number of messages. Graydon wants children to have an informed perspective on all forms of advertising. Because children are so bombarded, Graydon wrote a book, *Made You Look: How Advertising Works and What You Should Know*, to point out how pervasive ads are in our daily lives.

As a former public relations executive, Graydon has also helped develop a variety of promotional campaigns for big brands, including Kentucky Fried Chicken and Hasbro Toys, so she knows the secrets behind marketing and advertising.

Graydon says today more and more advertising is aimed directly at children. In North America, advertisers spend more than $2 billion a year on ads. That's because marketing experts estimate that young people in North America spend a staggering $100 billion every year on toys, clothes, video games, music, and other stuff. In her book, Graydon uses an analogy of a media mouse-

The average young person views about 40,000 ads on TV in one year.

trap—the cheese is the programs we watch and the TV ad is the mousetrap. Who's the mouse? Anyone of your students, that's who! The "cheese"—hot TV shows—attracts the mouse, who does not suspect that the ad trap is about to snap. And when it closes, it's closing on the family's wallet. Ouch!

You can teach students to distinguish between the ad messages and the informational reports in print or on TV. Students enjoy discussions of advertising as much as adults do. And admit it—advertising entertains all of us. Every year, millions of adults tune in to the Super Bowl to view the cool ads as much or more than the two teams fighting it out on the gridiron. Children are pretty smart at getting the advertising messages in those big-budget ads.

(continued on page 49)

Lesson Notes and Activity Materials

The activity "Keep an Eye Out for Ad Messages" will work best over a longer time period than as overnight homework. A week or a weekend will give students time to complete their observations.

Public Relations—or Ad?

Young people may have a harder time decoding or understanding the source behind a public relations message. Some of those messages have legitimate information, but you should teach students the concept of public relations—define it and explain it. It's worthwhile to take a few minutes in class to explain the functions of public relations, public information (public relations from our government agencies), and advertising as you help students learn to make the most of using media.

With advertising, you know the aim is to get your attention and to sell you a product. Public relations messages are legitimate ways to get information, as long as you know where the message is coming from and you verify it from other sources.

One of the main places young people encounter public relations messages is on the Internet. For example, if students are doing research and visit a university Web site for a story on their favorite college sports team, they will see a public relations story giving positive and helpful information on the team. Or when students get mailings on summer camps or newsletters from the school district, they're seeing public relations messages that highlight good things.

Media people work closely with public relations people, who not only offer story ideas but also are liaisons for setting up interviews, scheduling press conferences, and planning events. Public relations messages aren't bad—after all, you'll want to use them when you're sending out good news about your students. It's just important to know that the function of public relations is to offer the *good* news.

Patricia Orlowitz, a former public relations executive and now a public information officer with USAID, says, "Good public relations is valuable—I want to hear a manufacturer's idea about

The function of public relations is to offer the *good* news.

what are the advantages of its product, I want information about a company that I can find in the annual report, I want instructions on how to use a product. When a new product comes out, who knows it better than the company that developed it?"

But Orlowitz stressed that as a consumer, she would then search for other viewpoints and sources—the more the better—to be informed. She also says teachers should advise students to carefully check the credentials of the public relations source.☺

Expert Opinion

Shari Graydon is the former president of the media watchdog organization Media Watch and author of *Made You Look: How Advertising Works and What You Should Know.* She teaches student workshops on advertising and has also taught media analysis to college students.

Children are bombarded by advertising. What can they do to distinguish the hype from the facts?

The number one thing to keep in mind is that advertisers are trying to sell (you) something. For example, advertisers are trying to make every toy look like it's the most fun you could possibly have. They use special effects, lights, and music to make the toy seem more exciting.

Can you talk about other types of advertising, such as magazines, that are really only advertising sections in disguise?

Any time you go into a big movie theater, you can pick up a magazine produced by the theater that promotes future moviegoing. Everything in the magazine is positive. You'll never read a story that says "Don't go to this new movie. It's schlock; don't

waste your $10." Nothing in the magazine will be critical. The sole purpose is to encourage you to see all the movies promoted. Many companies, including drugstore chains and clothing manufacturers, create this kind of advertising to encourage people to buy their stuff.

More than twelve thousand schools across the United States and Canada use Channel One or YNN, the Youth News Network, in classrooms. But these networks do carry advertising. What does that mean for teachers?

Advertisers pay these specialty stations a lot of money to reach students. Educators sometimes object to these news pieces because they are too short to really teach students

anything and the advertising cannot be ignored…. Schools that use these networks can't put the TV on mute when the commercials come on.

Another problem with Channel One and YNN is that they are not independently produced news shows.

You're not going to see a news story carried on one of these broadcasts that could be negative to the sponsor. For example, if a snack food company were the sponsor, the broadcast wouldn't run a story on childhood obesity.

What about the popularity of wearing brand names? What can teachers tell students?

Tell them, when you're sporting a company's logo, you are free advertising for that company's products. It's not good or bad. It's up to you, but just be aware that you're paying 20 to 40 percent more to wear that company logo.☺

Sites and Sources

Made You Look: How Advertising Works and Why You Should Know by Shari Graydon (Annick Press) is an excellent resource for teachers. This student-friendly book is broken into chapters that cover the history, the marketing tactics, and the focus on young people of advertising campaigns. The book is loaded with activities that teachers can incorporate into classroom and homework lessons.

Graydon recommends these Web sites for teachers:

www.cme.org/cme .... the Web site of the Center for Media Education & Campaign for Kids' TV

www.mediawatch.ca .... the Web site for Media Watch, a nonprofit women's group that focuses on improving the image of girls and women in advertising

www.made-you-look.ca/ .... the Web site for Shari Graydon's book. Gives you more information on the author and her school programs.

Ad Watcher's Diary

Besides the obvious reasons advertisers give you to buy their products, ads also give you more subtle messages.

1. Join the crowd—don't miss out!
2. The product will make you cool or will make your life fun and exciting!
3. If the music is cool, the product must be cool—right?
4. Celebrity sports stars recommend it. You know they get paid a really lot of money for saying so—right?

Watch your favorite thirty-minute TV show and take notes on the products advertised. Use the chart below to record the products. Try to identify the subtle messages and write the message number from the list above.

Name of show _____

Product _____   Product _____

   Message _____   Message _____

Product _____   Product _____

   Message _____   Message _____

Product _____   Product _____

   Message _____   Message _____

Product _____   Product _____

   Message _____   Message _____

Product _____   Product _____

   Message _____   Message _____

Ace Advertisements

Pick up your favorite magazine and clip out an ad that catches your attention. Answer the following questions about the ad. Attach the ad to this sheet when you finish.

What is the product advertised?

Why did this ad get your attention?

Does it make you want to buy, or have your family buy, this product?

Do you need this product? Why or why not?

Will you remember this ad?

Name _____ Date _____

Keep an Eye Out for Ad Messages

Advertising isn't just on TV or in magazines and newspapers. Use this sheet to keep track of other places where you spot ads as you go about your activities for the next few days. Hint: You can count an ad as anything with a product or a company name (a soccer shirt that has a store sponsor or logo or a brand-name product in a TV show, not just in a commercial). List what you saw and where you saw it (on a billboard, on a bus, on clothing) in the space below.

Product	Company	Where Advertised
_____	_____	_____
_____	_____	_____
_____	_____	_____
_____	_____	_____
_____	_____	_____

With classmates, discuss these questions about the research you did.

1. Did any of the places where you saw ads surprise you? Which ones?

    _____

2. Studies show that people have to see a product advertised seven times before they will buy it. Do you think seeing all the ads you listed makes you more likely to buy those products? Why or why not?

    _____

Snappy Slogans

It's your turn to be an ad writer. You've talked in class about slogans—like "Just do it" from Nike or "I'm lovin' it" from McDonald's. Advertisers use catchy slogans to keep their products on your mind. Come up with three slogans for a new kind of sports shoe. If you want to, draw one sample ad showing your new product and using your best slogan. Notice that the slogans don't have to tell anything about the product.

Name of my new shoe

_____

_____

Advertising slogans

1. _____

2. _____

3. _____

Sketch your ad idea here.

Get the Picture

A picture is worth a thousand words.

You've heard that saying many times and in the case of photographs in the media, that's certainly true. For younger students just learning to use the print media, photographs are the first "reading" they do. The images tell young readers what is happening even before they develop the skills to read the story.

away. Sometimes the images aren't appropriate for children. There are some good magazines just for students. *Time* magazine's young-reader edition, *Time for Kids*, is a great educational tool (*www.timeforkids.com*). Another good resource is *Junior Scholastic* (*www.scholastic.com/juniorscholastic*). Both publications cover

page. Photo editors, however, do strive to show images that are memorable, compelling, and suitable for all readers.

Mike Smith, an editor at the *New York Times* and a veteran photojournalist, says, "Good photojournalists work very hard to capture images that reflect emotion while respecting the dignity of the people they photograph. It's hard work, and often the results are controversial."

Photos are fantastic tools for discussion.

Images tell stories, whether they're the moving images captured on film and video or the photographs on the pages of magazines and newspapers. Just as students first start with picture books in their reading selections, older students are drawn to the well-illustrated or photographed story in a newspaper or in a magazine. (And so are all of us!)

How can you use print media photos in the classroom? You can use them in your media selections and also as springboards to discussions.

News magazines such as *Time* and *Newsweek* are filled each week with fantastic photos, making places and faces real for readers, which is sometimes difficult when news is taking place far

important news with a young reader in mind, taking care to make the stories very visual but with images that are always appropriate.

Newspapers also have features for young readers in which special attention is given to the photo selection. For our own newspaper feature, Yak's Corner, we always keep in mind what is appropriate for children when covering news (*www.yakscorner.com*).

When it comes to using news stories in the classroom, the advantage of print media over television is to give you control of what you present to the class. You can pick which story and page you want to use. If you feel some of the content is inappropriate that day, clip stories from another

Photos are fantastic tools for discussion because the images are so personal and moving. Any story told with photos will likely leave more of an impression. Photos grab the readers' attention and pull them into a story.

There are also times when a newspaper or magazine produces a photo essay—a series of photos with very little text—to tell a story. *National Geographic* is a wonderful magazine to explore geography with young readers, thanks to the awesome photography. On the other hand, a community newspaper will also draw the readers in to follow photos of local places, of people they know—and even of themselves. Pictures tell great stories. Use the work sheets in this chapter to get your students to see the story behind the picture.☺

Lesson Notes and Activity Materials

For the "Your Story in Pictures" activity, give students a few days' notice to collect photos to bring. Try to make a photocopier available to them to avoid damage to photos.

Expert Opinion

Mike Smith is a veteran photo-journalist and editor at the *New York Times*.

He has been a photo editor at some of the biggest newspapers in the country, including the *Philadelphia Inquirer* and the *Detroit Free Press*.

What made you become a photojournalist?

I always enjoyed telling stories about people with pictures. Being a journalist gave me permission to meet people I would never otherwise meet and to drop in on their lives for a while to see what they're like. I also enjoyed seeing my pictures and stories published and being read by thousands of people.

What is the most controversial subject you've dealt with?

Often, photographs that depict suffering or pain or bad news are very difficult for readers to take, especially on the printed page, because the picture just sits there and looks back at you. Pictures of bodies in war or of people in very deep personal pain, such as relatives reacting to a murder or family members during a funeral, can be emotionally difficult for even casual readers of newspapers. Sometimes their natural reaction is to blame the person who took the picture, thinking that somehow the photographer delights in capturing these kinds of tragic scenes.

I can tell you that those pictures are the hardest thing a photojournalist has to do. But it is part of the job. Good photojournalists work very hard

to capture images that reflect emotion while respecting the dignity of the people they photograph. It's hard work, and often the results are controversial.

As a photojournalist and an editor, what are the factors that weigh in as you pick front-page photos?

Front-page pictures, in particular, should always reflect the important news of the day or give a significant visual point of view to an important feature or enterprise story that may not be, strictly, news. It's important to use restraint when a photograph is extremely dramatic but perhaps not terribly significant.

It's important to be fair in the kinds of people and situations that end up on the front page so that we don't give wrong impressions. If, for example, we cover a street protest in which 99.9% of the protestors are peaceful and orderly, but our picture shows one dramatic arrest with lots of tension, then to use that picture to illustrate the news might give a false impression of what actually happened.

Children are bombarded by all kinds of media. Do you have advice for teachers on helping students evaluate messages and think critically about what they read and hear?

Encourage them to always use their analytical skills. Don't accept at face value what someone else tells you or shows you. Ask lots of questions about how something is known

or why a particular person has the point of view she or he does.

If people can't tell you how or why they know something—and support it with evidence—then it probably isn't worth your time. If something looks true because it's printed on a page or looks stylish because it's on television or sounds pithy in an advertising slogan, ask yourself why. Is it because it's true—or just because someone wants you to think so? Listen to many different points of view, especially if they are not your own.

Analyze those points of view, and decide for yourself what is real or significant, true or not true.

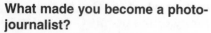

Learn to listen well. Think for yourself.

Where do you draw the line on what images should be shown?

The line is always moving. Often it's not the subject matter but the way in which the subject is depicted. I could argue that a photo of a dead American in the early days of the war in Iraq was an important photo to publish, to remind people that real men and women die in war and therefore we should be sure, as a country, that we make the right decision in putting those lives on the line.

On the other hand, a picture of a dead American, clearly identifiable to his or her family and friends, would cross the line (in my view) of what is acceptable. To print such a photo could cause unnecessary pain to the family and show a lack of respect, in general, to other soldiers and their families.

(continued on page 57)

Don't fail to live in the world you report on.

But the truth is, each situation is unique and must be evaluated on its own, in the context of the news of the day, the mores of the culture, the sensibilities of readers, etc. This is where and why analytical skills are so important and why listening to others is such a big part of the decision-making process.

What advice do you have for young people who want to pursue journalism careers?

Learn to listen well. Think for yourself. Ask the tough question. Ask another. When you think you've got it all figured out, realize that you probably don't, and ask some more questions.

Be open to criticism. It's how you learn and get better.

Learn new skills continually. You'll need as many as you can master.

Don't fail to live in the world you report on. Your life is just as important as the ones you write about and photograph. ☺

Sites and Sources

www.nationalgeographic.com .... the Web site of the National Geographic Society. Loaded with beautiful photos from the magazine for adults, as well as photos and stories from the family of publications.

http://yahooligans.yahoo.com/content/news .... a site for images of the hot news of the week for students. The site sorts through safe sites on the Web that also will give your students a wide range of interesting and newsy photos and links to other safe sites.

www.life.com .... the Web site of the classic *Life* magazine. It's a great source for wonderful photography. Visit the online archives to check out famous photos from the past and famous covers.

Your Story in Pictures

With the help of a parent or adult, gather pictures that tell your story. Include a baby picture, a toddler picture, and an early school photo. Plus include photos of you doing some of your favorite activities. Photocopies of the photos are fine. Paste them to the work sheet, starting with the baby picture at the top.

Write a Caption

Every picture in a newspaper or magazine has a caption—a line under or next to the photograph that describes what is happening and who is in the photo. In the box, paste a photo or photocopy of a picture that says something about you—a family photo, a holiday photo, a vacation photo, or a photo of you doing an activity you enjoy. Write a caption below describing what is happening and who is in the photo.

_____

_____

_____

_____

_____

The Story Behind the Picture

Captions tell a story. Look at the photo and its caption below. Now answer these questions about the photo.

What is happening in the picture?

_____

Who is in the picture?

_____

Where was this picture taken?

_____

Beyond the information in the caption, what other facts can you tell from looking at the photo? List three below.

BAYT AL-FAQIH, REPUBLIC OF YEMEN—Yemini women buy bread at the weekly Friday market.

1. _____

2. _____

3. _____

Lessons on the Run

Every teacher knows even the best-laid lesson plans can and sometimes should be changed. The attacks on the Pentagon and the World Trade Center on September 11, 2001, happened on a school-day morning. Most teachers of elementary students did not report the terrorist attacks. But in the following days, weeks, even months, the attacks shaped the daily news. Some schools arranged for speakers and assemblies to follow up on the news. Other schools took a proactive approach, organizing card and letter campaigns and fund-raising activities to help organizations such as the American Red Cross.

When big news happens, whether it's a tragedy or a crisis or a milestone in our country's history, teachers can use media as a classroom resource to help students better understand the world around them.

Every day, veteran Michigan teacher Barb Samra starts off the morning with what she calls factoids. On the chalkboard, she writes a question about a story in the local newspaper. Samra, who has been teaching middle school for more than thirty years, finds that a simple question will generate discussion and deftly demonstrate why her students need to learn their subjects.

She currently teaches science and thinks nothing beats a newspaper story for pulling together the concepts of science in action, along with geography, math, and language arts skills.

Samra says any story serves to strengthen students' critical-thinking skills. For example, when President Bush announced his goal to get the space program back on track, including a return to the moon with a goal of eventually heading to Mars, Samra's students not only looked at the science of Mars but had a lively discussion on the cost—roughly $130 billion to $250 billion. Many of these debates carry on at home, as well, which, Samra says, reinforces what students are learning at school.

It's key for teachers to be flexible and willing to abandon even the best lesson plan if a news event has captured the attention of your students. When dealing with disasters or difficult news, it's best to get the approval of your school administrator and find out the school policy. Often, after news has happened, schools are able to follow up with relevant lessons tailored to the age of the students. Many schools, for example, responded after 9/11 with a variety of age-appropriate assignments, including artwork and poetry reading, with classroom lessons emphasizing values of unity and patriotism.

Using different types of media helps students who have different learning styles. A visual learner will appreciate television or film lessons. A student who is an auditory learner may do well with books on tape or with radio broadcasts.

Teachers can use media as a classroom resource to help students better understand the world around them.

Dr. Kim Piper-Aiken, who teaches broadcast journalism at Michigan State University, reminds teachers that radio is a great medium for teaching. She is particularly a fan of National Public Radio. "Audio is another channel that can be very effective in terms of stimulating the imagination. When you don't have the visual channel, the audio channel works really well because it lets another part of the brain kick into gear.... When students listen, it's amazing how much they'll see because of that audio channel.... The more senses that we can engage, the better." ☉

Lesson Notes and Activity Materials

You will want opinion pieces from your local paper suitable for your students, including education stories and news about local government and the board of education.

Expert Opinion

Leonard Poger, a community-newspaper editor and writer for more than forty years in the metropolitan Detroit area, thinks community newspapers are an excellent tool teachers can use to boost students' skills across the curriculum.

Poger, who has visited many classrooms over his career, offers these ideas on how the newspaper—and other print media—can be used in your lesson plans across all subject areas.

Read All about It

Of course, the number one use of a newspaper is informational reading. As your students learn to use a newspaper, here are questions to test their reading comprehension that apply to every story.

- What is the reporter trying to relay to the reader?
- What is the topic?
- What is the main idea?
- What are some details that connect directly to the topic and main idea?

The Write Stuff

Second to reading comes writing. A community newspaper can be used to analyze major news stories, editorials, and columns for story organization and structure in language. Students can be assigned to write articles based on the facts found in any story.

Math Adds Up

Newspapers are packed with opportunities to use math skills. Using local sports stories, students can compute statistics in baseball (batting averages, runs batted in, earned run averages, and won-lost percentages). Using food stories, students can compare quantities when making recipes or learn to double or triple recipes.

Speak Up

By fourth or fifth grade, students are making oral presentations. Opinion columns and editorials are great practice for persuasive speaking. Find age-appropriate topics and let students take turns reading these columns out loud. Local papers, with topics covering schools and parks and recreation, are loaded with issues that can bring out the passion in your young readers.

Think about It

Local papers feature stories on issues your students can relate to. Find opinion pieces or editorials suitable for young readers and ask them to analyze and diagnose the content and consider other viewpoints on the same subject. Writing their own views forces students to consider other points of view.

Civic Values

Local newspapers carry news of your neighbors and school through human interest stories and education stories, as well as covering your city council or township board and your local board of education. Students can use this coverage to gain basic information about their city and school governments and how decisions that affect them are made by elected and appointed officials in the community.

Highlighting History

Local newspapers usually publish stories about local residents who were involved in historical events, such as surviving the Pearl Harbor attack that brought America into World War II. ☺

Some resources for fast lessons

- Web guides for teachers—Newspaper in Education departments of big papers. See Sites and Sources, page 64, for examples.
- *Chase's Calendar of Events*—Unique entries for each date cover historical anniversaries, international festivals, and unusual holidays for quick lessons. Information: *www.chases.com*.
- *The Teacher's* Calendar—more concise but still hefty volume by the editors of *Chase's*. Includes themes for special weeks and months.
- "50 Fun Things Kids Can Do with a Newspaper"—a collection of fifty cards with activities using the newspaper. Information, current pricing, and ordering: call 595-248-5385; online, *www.rcanderson .com/specialnie.html*.
- *Kids Discover* magazine—single-topic issues including space, weather, people, history, and science. A smart, well-designed magazine. Also produces teacher's guides. Information—call 212-677-4457 or online, *www.kidsdiscover.com*.

One Teacher's Use of the Media

Barb Samra has been teaching middle school in metro Detroit for more than thirty years. She has taught social studies, science, health, and physical education. In her years in the classroom, Samra has always made use of the media. She particularly likes to use newspapers because they're current and easy to use and they fit into this busy teacher's day. She is currently teaching science and offers these ideas for science lessons on the run.

Samra Factoids

Students in Samra's class know what to expect when she gives them a daily factoid to digest. "Some teachers call this bell work," says Samra, "but whatever you call it, it's great for getting the day going."

Science is in the newspaper every day, through weather stories, environmental news, and stories on medical discoveries and research. Samra gets a morning newspaper, and when she arrives at school she puts a factoid or two on the chalkboard. A factoid is an assignment for her students to find facts from a particular story that is in the news.

Here's an example: Samra writes a question about a newspaper story on the International Space Station on the chalkboard:

"The ISS is in trouble. Give the page and article name (headline) from section A1. Why is NASA concerned? What led to this situation? What could happen in February during the planned space walk? Give two risks on the ISS. What would you do?"

By asking students facts about a story, Samra makes sure students understand what they are reading.

Beyond that, she loves to ask the "what would you do" questions to work on critical-thinking and problem-solving skills.

"You can get into deep discussions" with these factoids, says Samra, who says she hears from parents that many of the discussions continue at home.

Interactive Initiative

Samra has also found that newspapers are loaded with ways for students to interact with promotional contests, writing contests, and letters to the editor. Through the years, her students have been recognized. One of her students even won a trip to the NBA all-star game in a *Detroit Free Press* contest.

Another time, her students sent in questions for a news-for-young-readers column. They also offered advice to younger students in a special section on standardized testing. Samra works hard to find opportunities for her students and says the payoff is enormous in the pride they feel in seeing their names or their school's name in print. Samra advises all teachers to look closely at their local newspapers because there are many chances for students to shine in print.

Wild about Weather

Weather predictions—on TV, in the newspaper, or on media Web sites—are something Samra loves to use in many ways.

She has students **keep journals,** recording three or four forecasts each day from different types of media and comparing the forecasts to the actual weather and temperature. That way, finds Samra, students learn

something beyond the hype of some of the weather broadcasts. It's also fun for students to track accuracy.

She also finds the weather forecast to be a great **geography builder.** She assigns students to find ten cities around the world on the map and record their weather forecasts for that day.

She guides students to **weather news stories**. For example, when her students read about the fires in California, Samra made sure they also read about the mud slides that followed. She helped them make the connections between the various environmental factors in these cause-and-effect stories.

Of course, **math skills** are essential when she asks students to figure out daily temperature averages and means. If you live in a cold-weather climate, as Samra does, it's always fun to track predictions for snowstorms. Students love to anticipate snow days, even if they seldom arrive.

Samra uses the Internet (especially sites she has checked out for good science material), including CNN or MSNBC news sites, but she finds the newspaper is a great hands-on resource. ☺

Four Fast Lessons

Sports Summary

Each day, the sports section has games stories. Pick a game and ask your students to read for detail and write a one- or two-sentence game summary.

World Weather

Ask your class to pick five cities from the weather page and write down what the highs and lows are for each city. Then have them find what country and continent those cities are in.

When Disasters Strike

When a big storm, fire, or earthquake happens anywhere in the world, it's an opportunity to teach about geography, history, and science. Have your students use newspapers and magazines the week the disaster happened to study cause and effect and to map out where and why the disaster happened. Often there is great need after a disaster, and there are always ways students can help, from having a bake sale to raise money for a world relief group or the American Red Cross, to sending simple care packages of supplies or cards and letters.

Environmental Impact

Teacher Barb Samra finds many environmental and health stories in the paper are great examples of why people need to learn about the science of our planet and how to take care of it. When an environmental story happens locally, or even internationally, students can clip stories that spin out of the event from a variety of media including news magazines such as *Time* or *Newsweek*, daily newspapers, and special science publications such as *Nature*. By reviewing a variety of sources, students will have a better understanding of what has happened.

After students read about the topic, ask them how it affects their lives in ways big and small. Discuss what solutions there are to the problems. Samra often uses the same questions journalists refer to as the 5Ws and H—who, what, when, where, why, and how—when asking students to think about the problems.

Sites and Sources

www.dnie.com .... the Detroit Newspapers in Education site

www.nynewsday.com/news/education/sbp/.......... the *New York Newsday* student site

www.nytimes.com/learning/index.html .... the Learning Network of the *New York Times*, for grades three through twelve; for grades three through five, go to www.nytimes.com/learning/teachers/snapshot/

www.usatoday.com/educate/home.htm................. *USA Today* online education resources

www.npr.org... the Web site for National Public Radio

www.tfkclassroom.com... *Time for Kids* lesson plans and reproducibles

www.cnnstudentnews.com..................................... CNN news for students with discussion points for teachers

http://edsitement.neh.gov..................................... the National Endowment for the Humanities site, with lesson plans and links to museums, libraries, and universities

www.kidscoop.com... NIE educational activities and teacher newsletter

People Profile

Every day you can find profiles of people—famous people or ordinary citizens—who are newsworthy. Different sections of the paper have profiles. Sports stars are profiled in the sports section; TV and movie stars are profiled in entertainment and features pages. Find a profile about an interesting person and answer the questions below.

Feature Section

People in the News

_____
Name of person in the news

Written by _____
your name

Sketch a picture or cut out a photo of the person and glue it here.

List three facts you learned by reading the story about this person.

1._____

_____

2._____

_____

3._____

_____

Does the story give you reasons to respect or admire this person? If yes, what are those reasons? If no, tell why not.

_____

_____

_____

_____

_____

_____

Wise about Words

Newspaper and magazine stories often introduce you to new words.

1. In the first column below, write several new words you find in a newspaper or magazine story. In the second column, write what you guess the meaning of each word is. In the third column, briefly write the dictionary definition of the word. How close were your guesses to the real meanings of the words?

2. Pick one or two of your new words and write sentences using them.

_____

_____

_____

word	my guess	dictionary definition

Get Your Message Out

Now that you've read about the media, here are some tips on getting out the good news from your school and classroom. Newspapers and local TV stations do love to report good news.

Put It in Writing (or E-Mail)

Whatever news you have, remember that editors and writers, like teachers, are busy people. They appreciate a short written notice or an e-mail about your school event, complete with a contact person and phone number. If you're sending them news after the event, it's great if someone has also taken a picture that you can e-mail or mail. Follow up on your letter or e-mail with a phone call a day or two later.

Time It Right

Events that get publicized are often ones that tie to something timely. The media loves to celebrate the season—every season. Editors are always looking for stories that are fresh and reflect different celebrations and events in your community. For example, newspapers often run stories tied to Black History Month or to Women's History Month. If you're planning something special, whether it's a guest speaker, a play, or a festival, editors like to know. You're offering them a fresh way to cover good news in your community, and they'll appreciate it. It's also a good way your school community can show its diversity, with different ethnic traditions and celebrations in which your students participate.

Newsy Reaction

Newspapers are always looking for fresh angles in the local community that allow them to follow up on a bigger state, national, or even international news story. If your students read a story and then respond with action, your newspaper wants to know. For example, if your class writes to troops overseas from your hometown or even creates care packages for the soldiers, that's a good item for the paper.

Think Big, Think Small

If you don't think your story is worthy of coverage in the *New York Times*, don't worry. There are plenty of other places that will be happy to report your news. You can try bigger newspapers in your community, but don't forget about weekly community newspapers. Weeklies make a point of cover-ing local news, especially school news.

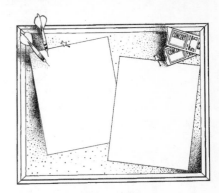

Advance Planning Pays Off

Just as you like to plan ahead on lessons, editors want to plan ahead on feature stories. When you have an event planned, big or small, let the newspaper or TV station know as far ahead as you can. A few weeks' notice is ideal. (Don't forget to put news of the event in writing and follow up with a phone call.)

Short, Sweet, and to the Point

Use a page from the reporter's notebook when you send in your news by using the 5Ws and H in a brief note. That means be sure to tell media outlets what students are doing, when your event is happening, who is involved, why the students are participating, where the school or event is, and how this event came about.

Get started broadcasting your news!☺

Lesson Notes and Activity Materials

Have students use the sample press release (p. 68) as a guide to prepare an announcement of an event taking place in your school or classroom. Or guide your students in preparing a press release as a class.

Name_____   Date_____

Sample Press Release

Dear Story Editor,

I want you to know about an exciting
event happening at Kennedy School next month.
Below are the details. I will call you next
week to follow up.

    EVENT: Literature Lock-In Party
     WHEN: Thursday, March 3
   WHERE: Kennedy School gym, Kennedy Street, Anytown, U.S.A.
      WHO: Kennedy 4th and 5th graders in Mrs. Booklover's class.
    WHAT: A Literature Lock-In Party to celebrate Read Across
         America Day. Students will dress as their favorite book
         characters and have a literature lock-in, spending the
         night at school with their favorite books. They'll have
         sleeping bags, refreshments, and flashlights for late-
         night reading. We plan to stay
         up late reading, as well as hosting a read-aloud and
         skits by parents, community celebrities, and staff.

  CONTACT: You can reach me, Ima Booklover, at school at 333-3333
         or at home between 6 and 7:30 P.M. at 444-4444, or by
         email at booklover@kennedyschool.

I look forward to talking with you about coverage for
this fun event.

Create a Classroom Newspaper

Once your students have learned how use the news, they can try their hand at creating a newspaper for your classroom. A classroom newspaper—even if it's only published once—is a great learning experience that puts all the lessons they've learned about media into play.

Assign Jobs

To start, you'll want to assign jobs to your students. You'll want to be the editor-in-chief; you can appoint editors in the following areas: news, sports, and features.

your students want to cover. We stress—"school"—not state or city for your first issue. When students start brainstorming, they'll find plenty of newsworthy topics to write about. Think like an editor in terms of beats—the cafeteria is one beat, the library is another, and someone can cover the principal the way a reporter covers the president.

Assign Reporters to Stories

When students have a list of good story ideas, work with the editors to assign reporters to the

how to assemble your newspaper. Many desktop publishing programs can put stories in layout formats. Check with your media specialist for guidance, or ask for parent volunteers to help with typing and layout tasks. If you don't have a lot of resources, a newspaper of typed stories, with simple headlines, is still a published work. Your students will be thrilled just to be in the paper or to be working on it. Print out copies for each member of your class and definitely one for your principal. If possible, print copies for each classroom. To help offset the cost of paper, you could sell your newspaper for a small fee (another lesson, this one in economics).

Someone can cover the principal the way a reporter covers the president.

You'll also need student reporters, columnists, and reviewers. If your paper is a success and you continue it each month, you may want to rotate the popular jobs. You also will want some artists and photographers. You'll know who in your class enjoys these activities. And, of course, you'll want parent volunteers. This is a parent-pleasing project, and you'll find parents who will want to help you—and their students—create this wonderful classroom souvenir.

Hold a Staff Meeting

To get started, hold an editorial staff meeting just like a real news-paper does. Brainstorm some of the stories at your school that

stories. (By the way, do make sure your principal supports this idea and that way won't be caught by surprise.) Students can also do profiles and polls relating to any of the topics. Help them format some features that could occur more than once, such as "Question of the Month" or "Student of the Month" or "Teacher of the Month." Sharing opinions is also popular. You may want to have students do a point-counterpoint opinion column on a subject such as playground rules, dress codes, or cafeteria menus.

Publish Your Paper

Once your staff has written and edited the stories, you can decide

Plan a Field Trip

Plan a field trip to your community newspaper or invite a speaker from your local paper to visit your class. Most newspapers have speakers' bureaus and encourage staff members to make time for young readers. Even if this is a one-time project, you'll have an im-PRESS-ive souvenir for your unit on using the news.☺

Lesson Notes and Activity Materials

Use the activity pages and graphic organizers on pages 71–80 to help students create content for a classroom newspaper.

Other Media Projects

Motivate students to write original, lively articles for your classroom newspaper. The worksheets on pages 71–80 can help them discover new ideas and organize their thoughts. The activities below are more ideas to help students experience media.

Read All about It

Students have many publishing opportunities in addition to classroom newspapers. Variations include a school newspaper, which serves the entire school, or a classroom newsletter, which is a short outlet for classroom news. Consider also posting the newsletter or paper on the school or class Web site.

Highly Classified

This activity will help students gain experience reading classified ads. Cut out appropriate help-wanted advertisements from the newspaper. Place the ads in a box and ask each student to randomly pick an ad. After students select ads, discuss the ads. Ask the class to identify and define the parts of a help-wanted ad: job title, description, skills required, start date, salary or wage, benefits, pension, resume, references, and cover letter. Compare and contrast various application instructions. You can complete the same activity using "for sale" ads.

School Features Brochures

Your school or class probably conducts special events, clubs, or services that could benefit from a simple brochure. Talk to staff from the music or drama department, media center, physical education department, or counseling services. A brochure can give students the chance to develop their publishing abilities.

Express Yourself

A literary magazine will give students an outlet for their creative writing skills, as well as the opportunity to publish a news report. Ask students from various classrooms and/or grade levels to submit stories, poems, essays, or other literary works. Student editors can select and edit the work, with teacher supervision. ☺

Name_____ Date_____

Reporter's Assignment

You are a newspaper reporter for your class paper. Your assignment is to write a feature article about a fun place for students to visit. Your article will appear in the entertainment section of the paper. Choose a place you enjoy or would like to visit. Use the questions below to help you gather and organize your information.

1. Who would want to read this article? _____

2. What is the article about? _____

3. What is the name of the place? _____

4. Where is it? _____

5. What are the hours (if any)? _____

6. What is the cost (if any)? _____

7. Children of what ages will enjoy this place?_____

8. Why is this place fun for children? _____

Write your article on a separate piece of paper. Use the form below to begin planning what you will include.

Headline

_____
title that will catch the readers' interest

Lead _____
introduces the story and usually includes one or two sentences that give the
most important details

Body_____
main part of the article that gives the rest of the details.
Put the most important details first.

_____

_____

_____

 0-7424-2736-6 *Using Media in the Classroom*

Use the 5 Ws

Complete the chart below to gather the information you need to write a news article. The article can report on a class trip or other event or activity.

Who	What	When	Where	Why

What sources will you use to find information for this article?

_____

_____

_____

Write one sentence that expresses the main idea of your article.

_____

_____

_____

List any photographs or artwork that might help readers understand your article. Attach a sketch of the artwork if necessary.

_____

_____

_____

Name_____   Date_____

Eyewitness Accounts

An eyewitness account often adds credibility and interest to a news story. When you interview someone about an event, it is important to collect all of the important information about his or her experience. Use this organizer to gather the information from an eyewitness to an event using these details.

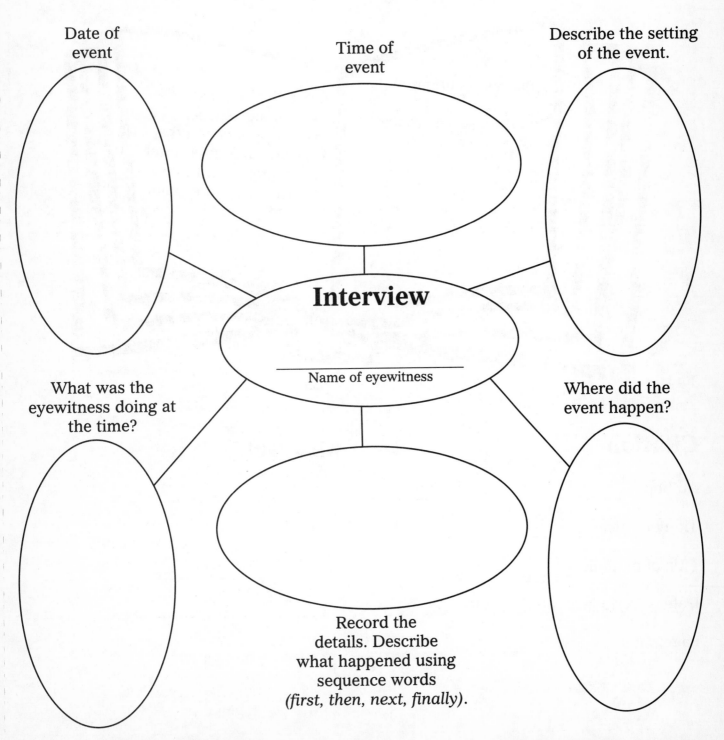

Date of event

Time of event

Describe the setting of the event.

Interview

_____
Name of eyewitness

What was the eyewitness doing at the time?

Where did the event happen?

Record the details. Describe what happened using sequence words (first, then, next, finally).

Name_____ Date _____

Periodical Abstract

An author writes an abstract to summarize the main idea and content of an article. When you write an abstract, mention the main idea of the article, as well as the most important points. Review the vocabulary words below. Then select and read a periodical article. Write an abstract for the article.

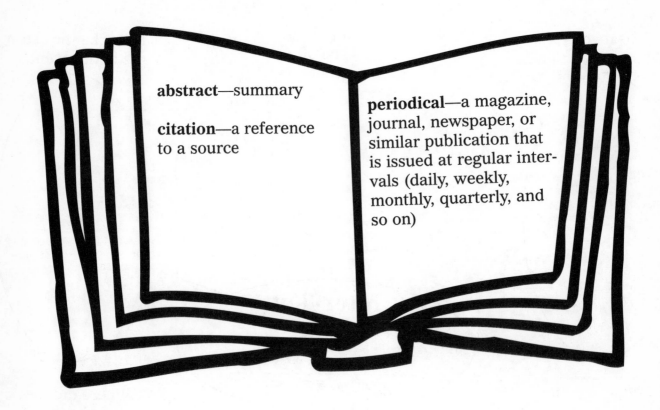

abstract—summary

citation—a reference to a source

periodical—a magazine, journal, newspaper, or similar publication that is issued at regular intervals (daily, weekly, monthly, quarterly, and so on)

Citation

Author_____

Title of article_____

Title of periodical _____

Date of periodical _____

Page numbers _____

Abstract

_____

_____

_____

_____

_____

Classified Ads

Merchandise

Homes for Sale

Sales

Think of an item you own that you would like to sell.

_____

_____

What features of the item would make someone want to buy it? Sketch below.

```
┌─────────────────────────────────────┐
│                                     │
│                                     │
│                                     │
│                                     │
│                                     │
│                                     │
│                                     │
│                                     │
└─────────────────────────────────────┘
```

What are some positive words you can use to describe the item? (But be truthful!)

_____

_____

_____

In which newspaper(s), magazine(s), or Web site(s) could you place your ad?

_____

_____

_____

For how many days would you run your ad?

_____

Write your classified ad. Include a description of the item, its price, and your contact information.

_____

_____

_____

_____

_____

_____

Name_____   Date _____

Upside-Down Pyramids

When reporters write news stories, they usually give the most important information first—the 5Ws. Then they give less important information. This way of writing is called an inverted, or upside-down, pyramid.

It makes good sense to write a news story this way. Readers want to know the most important information first. And news editors often have to make stories shorter to fit the space. The editor can cut from the end of the story to make it fit and know that he or she is cutting the least important information.

Most Important Ideas

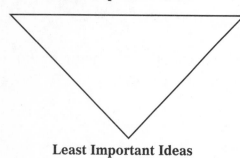

Least Important Ideas

Read the following news report and answer the questions below.

The President Is Shot

WASHINGTON, D.C.—President Lincoln was shot Friday night at Ford's Theater. Just days after the Civil War ended, John Wilkes Booth took his revenge for the South's losses. He stepped up behind Mr. Lincoln and shot him with a derringer. After the shooting, doctors carried Mr. Lincoln to a boarding house across the street. The extent of the President's injuries is not yet known.

1. Who? _____

2. What? _____

3. When? _____

4. Where? _____

5. Why? _____

6. How? _____

Prepare a news story for your classroom newspaper about a school event. Edit your story to put the most important information first. For example, report on a student council meeting—give the outcome of an important vote first, then fill in the details. For a sports story, first report who won, then give details of how that came about.

Words That Describe

Words that describe are called adjectives. They give the readers a clear picture of your ideas. They make your writing more interesting to read. Complete the phrases below. Use a different descriptive word in each blank. Do not use any word more than once.

Example: the <u>sharp</u> pencil
            the <u>yellow</u> pencil

1. the _____ balloon

the _____ balloon

the _____ balloon

2. the _____ truck

the _____ truck

the _____ truck

3. the _____ dog

the _____ dog

the _____ dog

4. the _____ man

the _____ man

the _____ man

Use words from the groups above to fill in the blanks.

5. The _____ balloon flew in front of the _____ man and his _____ dog.

6. The _____ dog sat in the _____ truck.

Name_____ Date _____

Restaurant Review

Pick a restaurant to visit, and then write a restaurant review.
Use the outline below to take notes.

Name of restaurant_____ Where is it? _____

Date and time I was there _____

Foods Ordered	Sauces, Spices, etc.	My Opinion

I waited _____ minutes to be seated.

How long I waited to order my food_____.

How long I waited for my food after I ordered_____.

Were the prices fair?_____

Any complaints? _____

My overall opinion _____

Would I recommend the restaurant to a friend?
Why or why not?

_____

_____

Name_____ Date_____

Movie Review

Write a review of the last movie you saw. Use the graphic organizer to gather your ideas and the movie details. Assume your audience has not seen the movie. Don't give away the ending!

Characters

_____

_____

_____

_____

_____

Setting

_____

_____

_____

Plot

_____

_____

_____

_____

Title

_____

My Reaction

_____

_____

_____

_____

Cast

_____

_____

_____

_____

0-7424-2736-6 *Using Media in the Classroom*

Sports Article

Write a news report on a recent school sporting event. Use this page to take notes during the event. When you write your article, begin with a strong lead sentence that tells who, what, where, why, when and how. Use colorful adjectives to describe the action. Use a thesaurus to help you find fresh but accurate descriptive words.

Sporting event _____

Location _____

Date and time_____

What were some of the most exciting things that happened at the event?

_____

_____

_____

_____

_____

_____

_____

_____

What did the individual or team do well?

_____

_____

_____

_____

_____

What could the team or individual have done better?

_____

_____

_____

Who won? _____

_____